Jesus Played Marbles

Written by Robert Haddad
Illustrations by Joshua Charadia

© Robert Haddad 2024

All rights reserved. No part of this book may be
reproduced or transmitted in any form
or by any means, electronic or mechanical, including
photocopying, recording, uploading to the internet, or by
any information storage and retrieval system, without
written permission from the publisher.

Published by Parousia Media Pty Ltd
PO Box 59 Galston, New South Wales, 2159
+61 2 8776 8778
www.parousiamedia.com
ISBN: 978-1-923131-80-4

Introduction

Sixty years before the birth of Jesus, the Romans, under General Pompey, marched into the land of Judea.

General Pompey came with many soldiers who, besides watching over towns and villages, had not much else to do.

To keep themselves from being bored, the soldiers played different games. One of these games was marbles.

Seeing this new game, many young Jewish children began playing marbles as well. This included the boys of Nazareth.

Nazareth

Nazareth was a small village in Galilee, to the north of Judea.

No one knows when people began to live there, but by the time the Romans came, there were a few hundred people living along its slopes.

Nazareth was not famous for anything special. It was even once asked whether anything good could ever come from there (Jn 1:46).

Yet we do know about one good family who quietly lived there. The father of this family was named Joseph; the mother was named Mary. They had one son named Jesus.

Joseph earned a living for the family by making furniture and fixing anything made out of wood or metal. Joseph taught Jesus to do the same. Mary loved both Joseph and Jesus very much and did her best to look after them every day.

Nearby lived the family of Clopas and Mary. They had many children. The boys were named James, Joseph, Simon and Jude. Sadly, we don't know the names of any of the girls. The boys often played together with Jesus. One of the games they played was marbles.

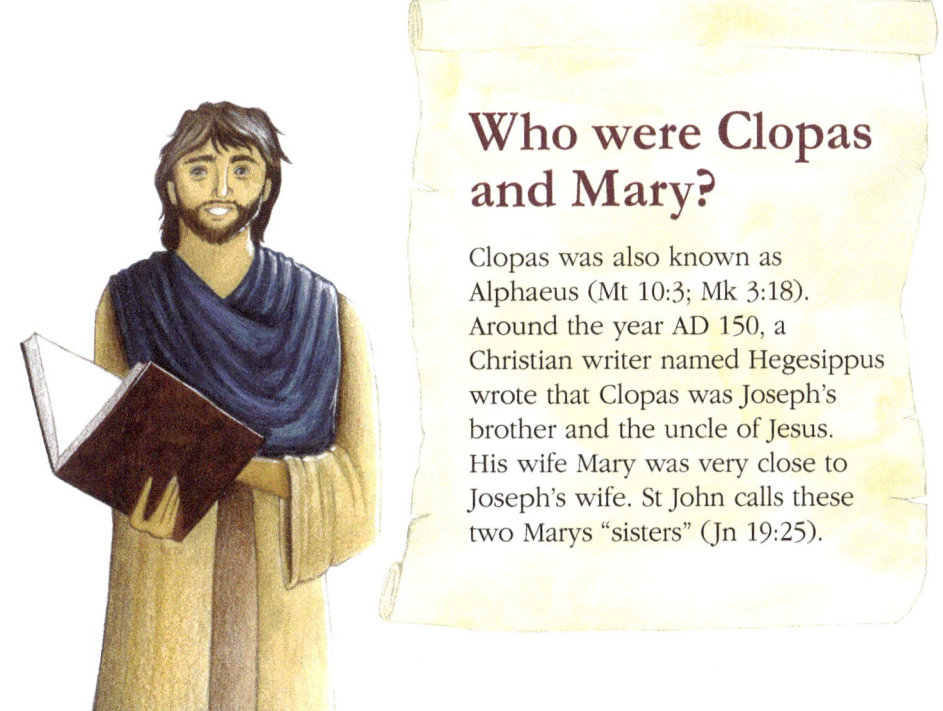

Who were Clopas and Mary?

Clopas was also known as Alphaeus (Mt 10:3; Mk 3:18). Around the year AD 150, a Christian writer named Hegesippus wrote that Clopas was Joseph's brother and the uncle of Jesus. His wife Mary was very close to Joseph's wife. St John calls these two Marys "sisters" (Jn 19:25).

Let's Play Marbles!

One day, the children of Joseph and Clopas gathered together. The boys were a little bored and wondered what they could do before it got too hot to play outside in the sun. There were different ideas:

"Let's play hide and seek."

"What about rock throwing?"

"How about bows and arrows?"

"I know," said Jesus, "Let's play marbles! I have six marbles in my pouch."

"Ok," agreed the others.

The game would be a simple one. The first person to flick their marble into the hole would be the winner.

After Jesus handed out the marbles, there was one left over. Who would get the sixth marble?

Joby

While Jesus was holding the spare marble he noticed another boy standing alone near the end of the street. This boy was known to everyone as Joby.

Joby came to live in Nazareth with his father about two years earlier. Because his mother was no longer alive and his father was often sick, Joby always walked around in old and torn clothes. Many times he had to beg for food and money so he and his father could eat.

This made Joby unpopular with most people in the village. Added to this, Joby could not see properly because he was cross-eyed. The other children would often make fun of him, calling him names – "Funny eyes, funny eyes, ha, ha, ha!" No one wanted to be seen with Joby. This made Joby very sad.

But with Jesus it was different. Seeing Joby, Jesus called him over. The other boys started complaining. Jesus said, "Joby, come on, here's your marble." Joby came closer, a little embarrassed. Jesus handed Joby his marble. The smile on Jesus' face made everyone fall silent.

James Goes First

Being the oldest in his family, James stepped up to go first. He had a green marble. He was confident because he had won this game many times before.

James flicked his marble high up into the air. It came down with a thud and just stood still without rolling any further. James was disappointed and stood behind the others with his arms folded.

Who was James?

James was the first son of Clopas (Alphaeus) and Mary (Mt 10:3; Mk 15:40). Because of his closeness to Jesus, he was called the "Lord's brother" (Gal. 1:19). He grew up to become one of Jesus' Twelve Apostles and be known as James the Less. He eventually became the first bishop of Jerusalem and played a very important part in the first council of the Church held around AD 50 (Acts 15). He also wrote a letter in the New Testament addressed to "the twelve tribes in the dispersion." Tradition tells us that James stayed in Jerusalem all his adult life and died there as a martyr in the year AD 62.

Joseph's Turn

Joseph was happy that James' throw was a bad one. Being the second oldest of the boys (Mt 13:55), Joseph was often in competition with James.

Joseph's marble was blue in colour. He was happy with it because it was larger than the other marbles. Being larger, Joseph could flick it harder and further.

Joseph's marble landed right next to the hole. Joseph was all smiles. Being closest to the hole meant that he would go first when it was time for second turns.

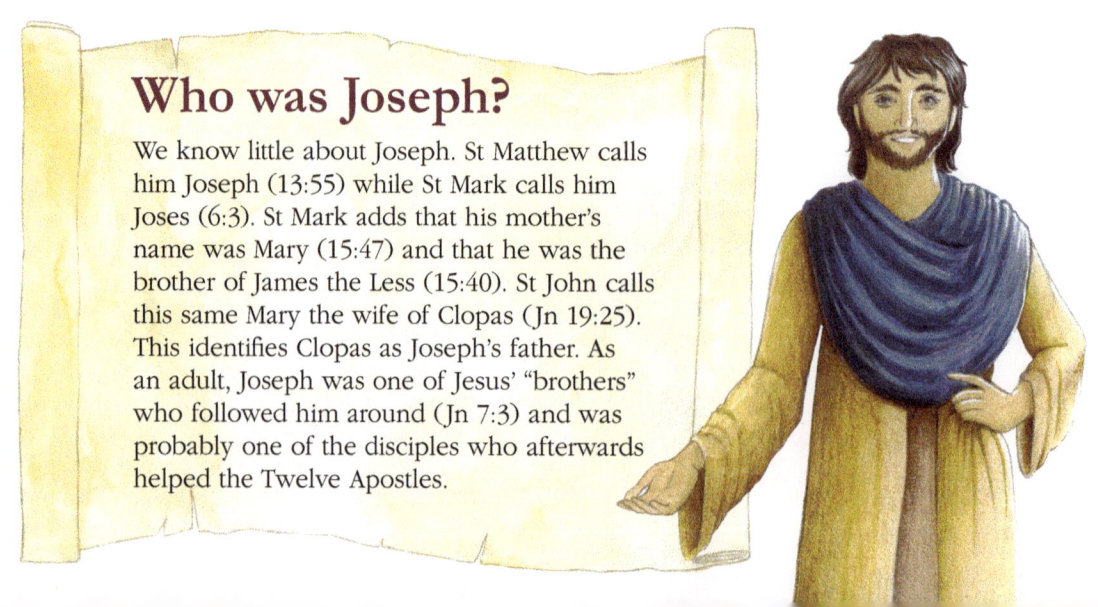

Who was Joseph?

We know little about Joseph. St Matthew calls him Joseph (13:55) while St Mark calls him Joses (6:3). St Mark adds that his mother's name was Mary (15:47) and that he was the brother of James the Less (15:40). St John calls this same Mary the wife of Clopas (Jn 19:25). This identifies Clopas as Joseph's father. As an adult, Joseph was one of Jesus' "brothers" who followed him around (Jn 7:3) and was probably one of the disciples who afterwards helped the Twelve Apostles.

Simon's Turn

Simon knew he was in trouble. Joseph's marble was too close to the hole. It needed to be knocked away. Was Simon good enough to do that?

Simon's yellow marble shone brightly in the sunlight. It rolled off his finger quickly and raced across the dirt.

Who was Simon?

We do not know much about Simon from Scripture. St Matthew (13:55) lists Simon as the third brother after James and Joseph; St Mark (6:3) lists him as the fourth brother after Jude.

Hegesippus again gives us more information. He says that Simon was the son of Clopas and became bishop of Jerusalem after the death of his brother James in AD 62. Simon remained bishop of Jerusalem until AD 107. He would live to over 100 years of age.

It looked as if it was going to crash into Joseph's marble, but missed and turned away to the right.

It stopped about two metres from the hole, the furthest away so far. Simon kicked the ground in disappointment.

Jude's Turn

After he finished laughing about Simon's bad luck, Jude walked forward for his turn.

Who was Jude?

Just like Simon, we are not sure whether Jude was the third or fourth brother, but we do know that, like James, he became one of the Twelve Apostles and as such was known as Thaddeus (Mt 10:3; Mk 3:18). Jude calls himself "a servant of Jesus Christ and brother of James" at the beginning of his short letter in the New Testament. Tradition tells us that Jude eventually preached the Gospel to many countries, including Syria, Armenia, Iraq and Persia, before dying as a martyr in Lebanon in AD 65.

Jude was a little nervous. As a younger brother, he was usually pushed around and not allowed to win any games. But because Jesus was playing with them this time, Jude felt a bit more comfortable.

Jude's white marble was the smallest but it was hard and strong. Rolling along the ground, it curved towards the left, passing James' green marble and resting a little behind Joseph's big blue one. Jude pointed to Joseph saying, "Don't think you will always beat me. Today is my turn!"

Joby's Turn

Joby stepped forward from behind Jesus. Some of the other boys began to grumble again.

"Why is he playing?"
"He is wasting our time!"
"Funny eyes, funny eyes, can you even see the sky?"
"Ha, ha, ha, ha…"

Catching Jesus' eyes, Joby felt encouraged. Looking at the hole, Joby flicked his black marble into the air. For a moment Joby lost sight of it because of the

glare of the sun. It landed on the ground and began to roll forward. To everyone's surprise, it stopped in-between Joseph's blue and Jude's white marbles.

Joby was happy but stayed silent. The other boys were silent also.

Jesus' Turn

Throughout the whole game so far, Jesus had said nothing.

The other boys were not worried about Jesus winning as he normally was very calm and didn't seem to get too excited about games. However, the serious look on Jesus' face meant that this time was going to be different. It was time to teach an important lesson.

Jesus came forward with his red marble. He knelt down on his knees and flicked towards the three marbles closest to the hole. Everyone held their breath as Jesus' red marble headed for the blue and white marbles and then bumped right into Joby's black marble. The force of the collision caused Joby's marble to roll right into the hole first.

This meant that Joby was the winner!

Nothing Else...

Everyone was silent.

James and Joseph had angry looks on their faces. Jude had his hand covering his face. Simon was mumbling the word "lucky" under his breath. Nobody except Jesus was happy that Joby had won.

Jesus then said, "Games are good, but the real winner is the one who shows the greatest love. For too long people have been very unkind to Joby, making fun of him and calling him names. I knocked his marble into the hole to show that Joby can also be a winner. Joby is just like us. He needs love too."

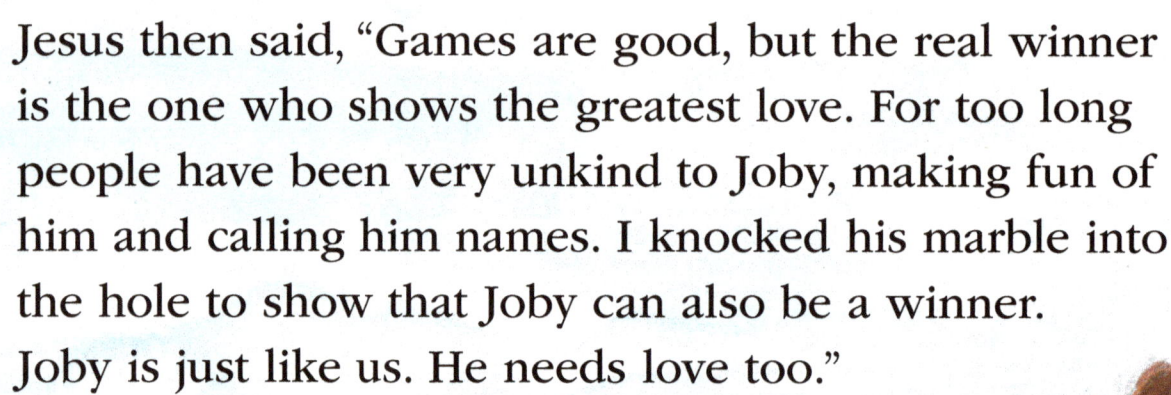

These words moved the hearts of the other boys. It was the first of many changes that would happen to them. They all came up to Joby and congratulated him, shaking his hand and slapping his back. Joby was overjoyed.

Joby then came up to Jesus and thanked him. Jesus invited him to have lunch at his house. As they walked away together, nothing further was said. It didn't matter. For the first time in his short life, Joby had felt the love of a true friend. Nothing else was necessary…

www.ingramcontent.com/pod-product-compliance
Lightning Source LLC
Chambersburg PA
CBHW042020090526
44590CB00029B/4344